Mastering OOP | SOLID Principles:

A Guide For Curiously Lazy Yet Smart Learners through real-world insights

Mastering OOP | SOLID Principles

A Guide For Curiously Lazy Yet Smart Learners

through real-world insights

ATIF A.EDEN

ISBN 9798858555537

Brief contents

Contents

Preface

A brief book that emphasizes the conceptual aspects of S.O.L.I.D principles with the four main pillars of OOP (abstraction, encapsulation, inheritance and polymorphism) with fantastic samples.

I've always wanted to see books more or less like the summaries I wrote from a session college.

Quite simply because just before the exams, I content myself with my summaries instead of revisiting all the course material. Rarely, if in doubt, I'll look in more detail in the course material.

By the way, I'm still adopting the same approach when reading technical books in all domains (programming, finances, personal development, etc.).

This method was and is still very effective and saves me a lot of time. Therefore, I have taken the initiative to write this book in a summary-like style. I wanted to keep things, at the same time, as light, as precise as concise as possible for you.

This book fills a gap in the IT book market. Indeed, the overwhelming majority of books dealing with such subjects are purely technical. In some cases, the reader cannot explain these principles aloud after reading these books!

Don't get me wrong. I'm talking about how the reader could implement the complex technical solution related to OOP and S.O.L.I.D principles, showing his code to his colleagues, and making a technical presentation to his teammates. But he can't make a projection in the real world explained with simple words.

However, this book, although short (on purpose), breaks this problem. In this way, the reader might be able to illustrate the main pillars of Object Oriented and SOLID principles easily.

Acknowledgements

I want to thank my parents, who taught me love and kindness.

My dear wife, Salma, thank you for always doing your best for us, your family. Our princess daughter and I love you so much! All of us are so grateful for having you! Thank you for all!

My two-year-old loving daughter, Tala, you are my ultimate inspiration. Besides you, I'm learning a lot about life.

Finally, I heartily thank you, beloved God. I owe everything to your kind providence, all my heartfelt gratitude.

About the author

Atif A.Eden is a senior cloud developer with more than twelve years of experience in Java. His day-to-day job centers on designing and building Java-based microservices.

When Atif isn't reading, coding, or writing, he lives with his wife Salma, and his daughter Tala, in Montreal, Canada.

During his free time, Atif workouts, chases after his daughter and reads books.

Atif can be reached at atifaeden@gmail.com.

Introduction

Regardless of the programming language studied, developers in training have necessarily seen the four pillars of object-oriented programming. Namely: abstraction, encapsulation, inheritance and last but not least, polymorphism.

Usually, the next step comes with advanced training or programming experience to highlight the S.O.L.I.D principles.

But how could we explain these complex concepts in sample words with real-world examples to developers and anyone else?!

You name it. The answer is in the remaining pages of this book.

Four main OOP pillars

1. Abstraction:

Imagine getting into a sleek, modern car. You slide into the driver's seat, eager to begin your journey. But wait a second—have you ever considered what's truly under the hood?

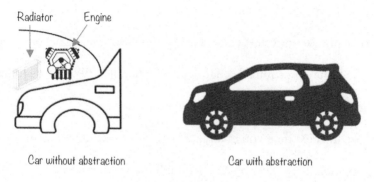

Car without abstraction   Car with abstraction

Figure 1: Abstraction in real-world

In the world of software development, abstraction is like a magician's cloak that conceals the complexities of what's going on behind the scenes, allowing you to concentrate on the task at hand. Just as you don't need to be an automobile engineer to drive a car, abstraction in programming allows us to interact with objects without becoming bogged down in the minutiae of how they work within.

Enter Java, one of the best innovation languages. In Java, abstraction is implemented using interfaces or abstract classes.

5

Picture it: the "car with abstraction" schema, in figure 1, becomes a blueprint, describing only the necessary actions like turning on the engine, accelerating, and shutting off the ignition.

But here's the secret: when you interact with this abstraction in your Java program, you're sheltered from the complexity that lies beneath. Want to start your car? Just invoke the turnOn() function. It's like having a reliable chauffeur who handles all of the technical details while you sit back and enjoy the ride.

So, the next time you marvel at the ease of starting your car, remember the power of abstraction. It's more than just driving; it's about opening up a universe of possibilities without getting bogged down in the technicalities. And, in the area of programming, abstraction is the key to unlocking innovation and increasing efficiency.

Encapsulation

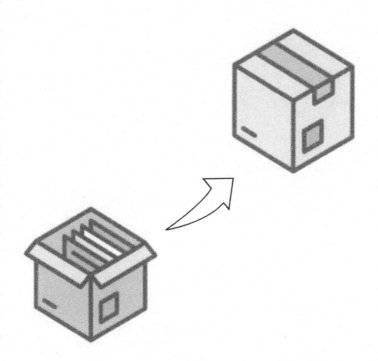

2. Encapsulation:

Allows you to control access to your object's state while making it easier to maintain or change your implementation later.

Here's below an accurate real-world illustration of that principle:

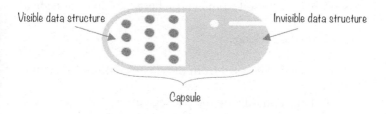

Figure 2.1: Encapsulation in real-world

The capsule in the figure above has two parts: a part with a data structure we want to expose (the transparent one) and a second part that we would choose to keep out of sight (the opaque one)!

In Object-Oriented Programming, in a language like Java, the Capsule would represent a class, and the data structure within it would be fields and methods. To restrict access to some data structures, we need to put them into the invisible part. We can accomplish this with only one access level called the "private" access modifier. Otherwise, we need to expose them to the visible ones. All members declared private are only accessible from within the same class.

Unlike the invisible part, we find several access levels in the visible one. The following access modifiers represent those levels:

- Public: Accessed from everywhere, within or outside a class or a package.
- Protected: Accessed from the classes within the same package and outside the package through child classes only.
- Default (friendly package): Accessed from non-child classes of the same package

Thus, we'll access the exposed data structure in the main program after creating a capsule object by instantiating the Capsule class. On the other side, the private fields and methods will remain sheltered from being accessed from outside by exploiting the "capsule" object.

Abstraction vs. encapsulation

2.2. Abstraction vs. encapsulation:

That being said, when it comes to abstraction and encapsulation principles, they look like the same principle, aren't they?

Figure 2.2.1: Abstraction vs. encapsulation

Well, this could be confusing as both pillars have a hidden part in the code. However, they are pretty different from each other.

Remember that abstraction doesn't focus on the inner workings. Instead, it focuses on the outside viewing (exposing). At the same time, besides the fact that encapsulation focuses on internal working or inner viewing, it is all about accessibility.

Furthermore, in java, abstraction is supported with interfaces or abstract classes, while encapsulation is supported using access modifiers like public, private, etc.

Inheritance

3. Inheritance:

Allows you to create class hierarchies, where a base class gives its behavior and attributes to a derived class. You are then free to modify or extend its functionalities.

Parent   Child

Figure 3.1: Inheritance in real-world

Inheritance is a straightforward concept and the easiest to understand. Basically, a child won't acquire 100% of his parent's character, behavior or appearance. However, he would receive a good part of his parent's properties.

In Object-Oriented Programming, The Child would be a class that extends the "Parent" one. This means the Child class will inherit the whole methods (behaviors) from the Parent one.

However, the purpose of creating a Child class is often to keep the common behaviors and have some additional specific properties and behaviors that distinguish it from the Parent one. This is like in real life, where kids are not identical to their parents.

This would seem harsh from a coding point of view, but we can achieve it by overriding the methods within the child class. Like this, we will change the method's behavior to fit the specificity of the Child class that we are looking forward to implementing. Notice that in java, there are two main keywords, "extends" and "implements" which are used for inheritance. Both serve almost the exact mechanism by which a class can inherit the features of the other.

4. Polymorphism:

Polymorphism ensures that the proper method will be executed based on the calling object's type.

First of all, The word poly means "many" and the word morph means "form", so when we talk about polymorphism, we're talking about something that appears in many different forms. The best example for nowadays polymorphic concepts is the Covid-19 variants!

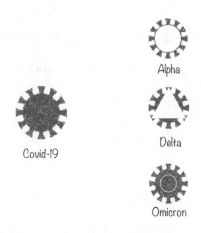

Figure 4.1: Polymorphism in real-world

We all agree that when a new variant appears and takes over. We always keep talking about Covid-19, rather than the variant itself, whether Delta or Omicron.

In Object-Oriented Programming, Covid-19 will represent the main class that the Alpha, Delta and Omicron ones will extend. Each subclass variant would have methods like infect(), getSymptoms() and so on! Therefore, each subclass would have a different implementation defined by the infection rate, symptoms, etc.

This being, and depends on the period of the pandemic, when someone is affected, he would rather say, "I got Covid-19" than "I got Delta" or "I got Omicron". Let's suppose that we are in the "Omicron" era, in java if we call the getSymptoms() method on the covid19 object we will get the omicron symptoms.

This means that we are talking about the general concept of covid-19 without diving into the details of the implementation (variants).

S.O.L.I.D principles

Single Responsibility Principle

5. SRP (Single Responsibility Principle) :

A module should have one and only one reason to change.

Let's consider the following multi-tool pocket knife:

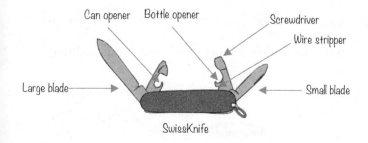

Figure 5.1: SRP violation in real-world

Generally, this kind of tool contains, among other things, a knife blade, a can opener, a wire stripper, etc.

Now, let's assume that the swiss knife is shared by different family members. What if the father would like to sharpen the large blade in order to make it handy for cutting things? And at the same time, the son needed to use the screwdriver for his DIY project, but he noticed that it was bent after several uses and needed to be repaired and so forth. Here the father and son are considered as two actors that want to make a change on the same tool for two different reasons.

Hence, as we can see, the swiss knife has more than one reason to change coming from different actors. In order to avoid this SRP violation, we need to extract different tools from the swiss knife and separate them from each other, as shown in the following figure:

LargeBlade   Screwdriver   CanOpener

Figure 5.2: SRP in real-world

In Object Oriented Programming, the SwissKnife class is now split into separate classes: LargeBlade, ScrewDriver, CanOpener, etc. In this way, every class of those will have one and only one reason to change by one actor at a time. For instance, no one would make a change on the screwdriver because the large blade isn't sharpened enough as They are both distinct and separate tools, as opposed to the Swiss knife, which is an all-in-one tool.

Open-Closed Principle

6. OCP (Open-Closed Principle) :

Software entities (classes, functions..) should be open for extension but closed for modification.

Let's consider the following hand blender tool :

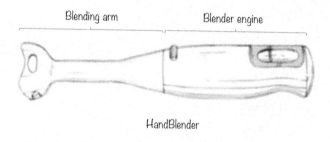

HandBlender

Figure 6.1: OCP violation in real-world

This is an excellent tool for so many uses, smoothies, soups... But what if we want to prepare a cake and whisk some eggs using the same hand blender for that new recipe?

Instead of changing the blender engine, we can change its attachment, the blending arm, with the appropriate equipment, in this case: a whisk.

To illustrate that, here's a figure with a hand blender that supports different arms (extensions): The blending arm, the whisk arm and the cutter arm. This hand blender will not change for real as the blender engine is kept for whatever use. Like this, we can say that the hand blender is open for extension but closed for modification (the blend engine base remains intact).

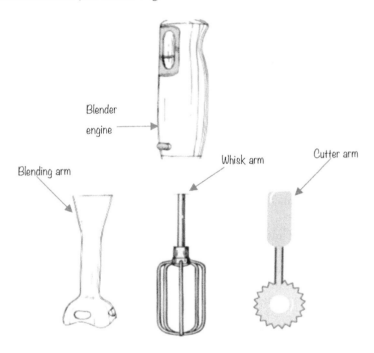

Figure 6.2: OCP in real-world

For instance, if we combine the whisk arm with the blender engine. We will get a different hand blender that serves to whisk eggs!

This way, we can say that the whole tool has been changed only by changing the arm extension without modifying the blender engine.

In Object-Oriented Programming, the classes BlendingArm, WhiskArm and CutterArm will extend a generic class: "Arm" and redefine the behavioral functions appropriately. For example, the abstract class or interface "Arm" will have an abstract method called "blend()". The WhiskArm class will override the "blend()" method and make it whisk eggs. The same thing for the BlendingArm that will make the "blend()" method pureeing soups, etc.

Liskov Substitution Principle

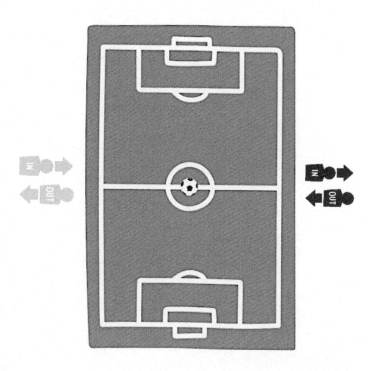

7. LSP (Liskov Substitution Principle) :

If for each object:

➢ **o1** of type **S**, there is an object

➢ **o2** of type **T**

such as the behavior of all programs "**P**" remains unchanged when

o1 is substituted for **o2** then **S** is a subtype of **T**.

Based on the definition, the LSP seems to be a highly complex

principle, but it's not. Let's dive into our real-world sample to make

things simple.

Figure 7.1: Hand blender
tool

Figure 7.2: Electric milk frother tool

Let's suppose that we were working on a soup recipe, then, for

some reason, the illustrated hand blender (Figure 7.1) was missing

in the kitchen. We looked everywhere but to no avail!

Then we came across an interesting idea, let's use a very similar tool in our disposition that might come in handy to continue our recipe. Take a look at the milk frother tool illustrated in (Figure 7.2)

The question is, could it be really helpful when it comes to finishing our recipe blending?

Obviously, the answer is NO. Hence, even though the hand blender and the milk frother look similar, they cannot substitute for each other (we cannot blend soup ingredients with a milk frother, right!). That use case is precisely a violation of LSP!

In order to respect the LSP in that case, we can use the kitchen appliance illustrated in figure 7.3: a blender!

We all agree that even though the blender has a different shape and form compared to the hand blender, it remains an excellent substitution to accomplish all the tasks that we usually do with one or the other.

That being said, let's revisit the LSP definition once again with a little update regarding the highlighted variables:

Figure 7.3: Blender tool

Objects: **o1** and **o2** [handleBlender and blender]

Types: **S** and **T** [HandleBlender and Blender]

Program: **P**

This Object Oriented Programming definition will follow:

If for each object:

➢**handBlender** of type **HandBlender**, there is an object

➢**blender** of type **Blender**

Such as the result "**get a blended soup**" remains unchanged

when **handBlender** is substituted for **blender,** then **HandBlender**

is a subtype of **Blender.**

Interface Segregation Principle

8. ISP (Interface Segregation Principle)

Clients should not be forced to depend on methods they do not use. Let's walk through this again in the real world. Let's consider the following multi-charging cable :

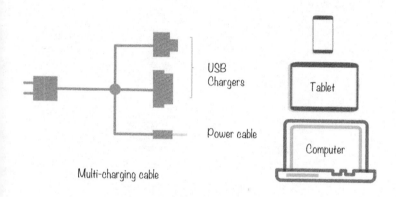

Figure 8.1: ISP violation in real-world

Let's assume that in order to charge our personal computer, we will use the multi-charging cable shown in figure 8.1 above. In such a case, we will have additional useless functionalities (other USB chargers). Well, this is a violation of the ISP!

To fix this, we need to make sure that each user gets the feature he needs, nothing more and nothing less. Don't get me wrong. I'm not trying to convince you that a multi-charging cable is a bad

invention. I'm just trying to give you an example from the real

world compared to object-oriented programming logic.

So, we can split the multi-charging cable into different charging

cables as below :

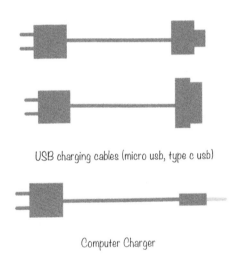

USB charging cables (micro usb, type c usb)

Computer Charger

Figure 8.2: ISP in real-world

Hence, in Object-Oriented Programming, the Computer, Tablet

and Smartphone represent classes that depend on the

MultiChargingCable class that comes with three separate

Methods or functionalities: phoneCharger, tabletCharger and computerCharger as illustrated in figure 8.1.

However, we don't want the computer to depend on something that carries additional features.

The solution is illustrated in figure 8.2 with separated cables, so the tablet will have one and only one feature from the tabletCharger, same for the computer and the phone (No more unnecessary additional features).

Dependency Inversion Principle

9. DIP (Dependency Inversion Principle)

High-level modules should not depend on low-level modules. Both should depend on abstractions. Abstractions should not depend on details. Details should depend on abstractions.

Here by abstractions, we mean interfaces or abstract classes, and by details, we mean concrete implementation. Let's consider the following example :

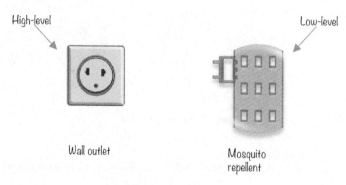

Figure 9.1: DIP violation in real-world

Obviously, by connecting the mosquito repellent to the wall outlet, the latter gets direct access to the mosquito repellent and becomes readily aware of it (tight coupling)!

We can prevent this by adding an intermediate plug, so the wall outlet cannot see what is connected to it except the plug itself! Let's

take a look at the following example :

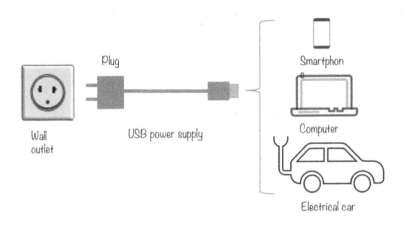

Figure 9.2: DIP in real-world

As you can see here, the wall outlet (high-level) only recognizes

the USB power supply connection, not what comes behind it (low-

level): a smartphone, computer or even an electric car! In this way,

the wall outlet depends on abstraction, not details.

In Object-Oriented Programming, the class or module WallOutlet

by depending on abstraction (USBPowerSupply), the design

becomes more flexible as we can plug indirectly any

USBPowerSupply implementation (ElectricalCar, computer,

smartphone, etc.) without changing anything in the WallOutlet

class or module, which means no rebuild or deployment for the

WallOutlet.

Thank you

Thank you for picking up this book and reading it to the end. I sincerely hope it met your expectations, and offered you valuable insights and knowledge along the way.

Before you leave, I would like to ask you a small favor. Could you spare me a few moments to leave a review of this book on Amazon? Your feedback is invaluable to me. It will shape the direction of my writing style, ensuring it aligns perfectly with your expectations.

So, if you found this book enlightening and appreciate the unique approach I've taken, please consider leaving a review. Your support is of great importance to me.

Thank you for your time, and I genuinely hope you enjoyed this book.

References

Martin, R. C. (2018). Clean Architecture: A Craftsman's Guide to

Software Structure and Design. Pearson Education, Inc.

Your Next Journey Is Here: Microservices made simple!

Are you prepared to transform your comprehension of software architecture? Take a look at "Come Shop with Me: Discovering Microservices One Store at a Time" to learn more about microservices and have your questions answered! Imagine browsing a busy mall where every shop reveals a fresh insight into contemporary software design. This is more than just a book; it's an exciting adventure that breaks down difficult tech ideas into manageable, human experiences. Whether you're an expert coder or just a curious beginner, our method will captivate you. Prepare to experience microservices in a whole new way! Now is the perfect moment to go shopping and immerse yourself in the cutting edge of software architecture!

65912040R00046